Yet Another Slice of Passion

The Continuing Poetry
of **Andrew Allen Smith**

Any event, person, place, or thing mentioned in the prose and poetry that follow may be based on real items. Names have been changed where necessary to allow for anonymity.

Copyright © 2025 Andrew Allen Smith

All rights reserved.

ISBN: 978-1-7340960-6-4

LOC: Pending

Contents

The Author and a Quest for Passion 1

Poetry 3

   A Warm Moment 6

   Static System 7

   The Night Goes On 8

   T'was the night 9

   Perhaps 11

   There's a Crack in the Sky 12

   The Way 13

   Amazed 15

   Obscure Piece 16

   The Embrace 18

   A new feeling 19

   Her Eyes 20

   Happy Without Tomorrow 21

   I will be 22

   Death and Love 23

   Life 24

The Night Goes On	25
The Point	26
I Took a Journey	27
WooHoo	28
Feathers and Scales	29
Awe	30
Walking Wild	32
It's about you	33
Look away…	34
Another Day	36
Purely Passionate Purpose	37
What is it?	38
I Missed You	39
Broken Science	40
Incessant	43
Look away…	44
Justice	46
Tearcicles	48
Just for Me	49
Shadows of Passion	50

Bitter Passion	51
Timberfall	52
That Moment	53
Breathe Deep	54
Understood a little	55
Already	56
Driven	58
Posted Life	59
The Mountain	60
Angrily	62
Time for a Nap	63
Awake Now	64
Battle	65
Across a Universe	67
The White Tower	68
How many sunsets?	69
Collapsible	70
At the Core	71
Check It Out	72
Colors	73

Touch	75
99	76
Rolling	77
Drain	78
AI	79
Reasons	80
Beyond	81
What cost	82
Undone	83
Spree	84
A time in the middle	85
Strong	86
Why	87
Sweet	88
Dark sounds	89
Paradox	90
Timeless	91
Why ask why?	92
Higher	93
Clumps	94

Leverage	95
Spoons	96
Silence	97
Not quite the stars	98
Wish	99
Pluralized	100
Foci	101
Inside	102

Footnotes and Follies ... 103

I Took a Journey	103
It's about you	103
I Missed You	104
Inside	104
Leverage	105
Sunsets	105

About the Author ... 106

Other titles available by Andrew Allen Smith: ... 108

The Author and a Quest for Passion

This is my third volume of poetry. Even with the number of poems that are in the three volumes, it doesn't touch the surface of the poetry that I have written. It's actually pretty funny, I have been writing poems since I was about 9 or 10 years old.

I remember at that time being in a class and walking through different types of poetry with the teacher. The idea of the rhythm fascinated me, and I often found myself thinking in stanzas as I wrote and tried to fill up my notebooks. How was I to know that it would eventually progress into a passion and perhaps beyond.

As my poetry progressed, I found that I was writing about more complex issues. Often, I would get lost in a feeling and even in a word. That's the way things can work when the words start flowing. I sometimes found myself changing word after word looking for that perfect series that would echo the 1212123 of a particular type of poetry. I also explored dictionaries and somehow got a hold of a book full of synonyms and antonyms and in the process I grew.

The question should be, "what motivates a poet?" and the answer, in my opinion should be "what doesn't motivate a poet?" As I grew and my poetry took on more complex situations, I found that everything was motivational. I read many authors and was fascinated by Edgar Allan Poe. His verse was sometimes repetitive and sometimes not, he stuck to no particular type of poetry, and I found myself drawn to his writings. While I opened my mind to further research, I found numerous writers that were similar. As poets they slid in and out of particular methods and often went completely on their own and created a new method to somehow incite passion and emotion.

A poem is not like a story, there are not an unlimited number of descriptors and chapters that paint a picture of an entire situation. Instead, a poet has to create a vision with a myriad of words that build emotions that cannot easily be written in just verse. There are words in poetry that are immortal and there are words in poetry that are lost, but when they are read once more, they always find a way to open the mind and the heart.

      Here I sit once again, sharing a part of my soul and once again I will find a way to incite and inspire with fewer words and a key to the most unlimited place I can find, the imagination. Thanks for picking this book up and going on a journey with me, not necessarily to anywhere but instead to everywhere. I hope you enjoy it, but mostly I hope at least one poem opens your mind to possibilities and maybe a little more. Passion will follow.

Poetry

There it was, lying before me. It was a poem that meant something, trying to mean something, and someday to mean something. That poem called out to me and wanted to be real like so many poems around the world. Somewhere in that poem, I found myself, and the poem found me. It was like we were never apart and always together, and it just belonged.

I suppose my first experience with poetry was very young and with very silly books. Even when people write poetry, we find ourselves fighting with things like children's singing songs versus and the lack of real substance. I was given a few books, and, in those books, I started finding the real power behind poetry.

It may sound somewhat cliche, but Edgar Allan Poe really called to me. It wasn't just his poems but the series of verses that he wrote, and the short stories and stories played with your imagination using words that could elicit emotion as well as vision. Those strong emotions carried on as I started to read the mini verses that were in publication and I found myself fascinated by this art that seemed to follow no particular pattern, no particular rule.

I wasn't the strongest in English for a while. Of course, I spoke it well as I grew up in the United States, but the dynamics of the language and the concepts and ideas can be pretty complicated if you pay attention to the rules. I wanted to pay attention to the rules and make things right, but I was not a memorizer, i was a thinker. I felt deeply, but communicating those feelings was very hard for me and my lack of a permanent residence until I was 15 made it even harder. Worse, even though we found ourselves in a city for more than nine months, we didn't necessarily have a home there either. Inside that city over a course of three years I lived in four different houses.

Somewhere in the midst of it all I started seeing the world a little differently. When I was a sophomore in high school, I started taking Latin and it was there that I started realizing that the verse in poetry did have structure and meaning, and it took a foreign language to teach me that. I became fascinated with the patterns that Virgil used and as I translated, I began to understand that no matter what language you are in there is a possibility of putting yourself out there with poetry and prose.

Although I had been scribbling down words and ideas since I was about eight, many of them were intertwined with mathematics and engineering concepts. Movies and books played a part in opening my mind to the world of possibilities, and my grandfather, a professor of mathematics, somehow gave me the insight to know that math was a part of everything, and the patterns of math were as eloquent as any poem. As I find many of these writings in journals and slips of paper I am trying to translate and understand the emotions I was feeling. It is sometimes difficult for me to understand because even though I remember everything vividly, I wonder if that was who I was or if I am interpreting by who I am now.

I kept reading and trying to improve my spelling and understanding of the concepts of the English language, even though they are quite ridiculous sometimes. As I did so my writing got better, and I was fascinated and amazed by how I could reread a poem and feel the depths of what I was feeling when I wrote it. I didn't always share those poems, but I held them close to my heart, simply because they made me somewhat safe.

The home I had found in the inner city was also a prison. The rules from all the cities I had lived in before were now gone, and this new town was very different. My communication had to be modified and all I wanted what's to find someone that would feel with me and experience the passion and depth that I felt. I believed and still believe that there are those people that are so in depth with their empathy that they will give their all to someone and their perfect companion is someone that will give everything back to them and in the process create a love that just cannot be broken.

I have collected a significant number of volumes of poetry. As I did so I found a little bit of peace in the words that someone else had put on a page and found kindred spirits who were looking for that passion but could not find it or could not experience it.

As we walk through the pages, I can only say that the world is a fantastic place and all you need to do is believe in finding the passion necessary to write a poem. It may not be the best in the world, but if it is from your heart that is all you need. Believe in yourself and enjoy the poems that I have written that brought out passion in me or let me experience a world that was better simply because I felt it.

A Warm Moment

Do I ask too much?
all I would like is a warm moment to share the world
all I would like is a piece of time to share the experience
all I would like is a soft hand to hold in mine
all I would like is the world

Do I see too much?
all I would like is a clear vision of today
all I would like is open eyes by more than me
all I would like is to see kindness that is real
all I would like is to find my eyes opened by truth

Static System

I think I found a path
it may not be easy
but it is a path that may make my world's more clear

I think I know a way
it is an amazing way
but it is a way that may be filled with uncertainty

I think I found the secret
it may be well known
but for many it is a choice they do not follow

I think I'll be OK
that's all that's important
and only I need to hold on to this knowing

I think the world is static
I know it may not be true
but the constant drone drowns out all I hear

I think I sense the best
others may not see it
but I know that there is some of it in us all

I think I will find peace
even though it may seem different
but my peace may be another man's chaos lost in the static

The Night Goes On

It was a simple moment driving tonight
a simple moment that felt so right
I passed the car then two then three
I wasn't sure why it was me

I drove farther and faster then slower and more
I kept on driving and tried to explore
the day became knight and the night was fun
for after all the night always goes on

I drove for a while and didn't feel tired
I just kept driving and I think I was wired
it wasn't a bad night nor was it good
I just kept driving because I knew that I should

and finally it came my destination was here
and not even once did I even feel fear
the day became night and the night was a song
the song kept repeating that the night goes on

I sit in my bed now about to fall asleep
I don't know whether to laugh or whether to weep
I went far and wide and hither and yon
and all the while the night goes on

T'was the night...

T'was the night before Christmas, and all in the land
Not a creature was stirring, except writers hands
While other sat silent tucked well in their bed
Imaginations ran wild, and filled writers heads
The worlds were fired, and full of sheer chance
and waited for no one to do their strange dance
When people woke up and looked on in worry
Writers just laughed and said they would hurry
Two moments had passed and then a whole night
Our writer was lost in another plot plight

When words collided and none could be found
Often the writer would lay his head down
then down from the chimney or easel or fare
would come a fun person, with no rhyme and no care
A thought for a writer or actor or two,
a positive moment that would last the night through
The laughter was real and it shattered the silence
and no one could fathom the sound they heard since

"On laughter, on giggles, and smile for a moment
no judgement no fear now, the feelings he sent"
and always some cried, "it is a lie and not true"
but the laughter continued for me and for you
and when writer and actor and artist awoke
they shook their heads sideways and thought it a joke
The ideas were teaming from a few words so kind
that suddenly the block they had felt would unwind

Ideas now flowed from the writers with care
and artists were happy and their souls they did bare
For those not affected by writing and more
The sound of the laughter they too did adore
It's time to let go of a block or another

and laugh with you all as a friend and a brother
For whatever you feel, and what you may do
Merry Christmas and holiday wishes for you

Perhaps

perhaps they missed the plush chair reflected in the background waiting to be sat in
perhaps they missed the two statuesque ghosts floating carefully to their side watching all that they did
perhaps they missed the infinite panes of glass behind them watching like silent sentinels
perhaps they missed the cascading steps going everywhere and nowhere
perhaps they missed the art behind them by a forever artist forgotten for never more
perhaps they missed the winning hand held high with the ace in the hole
perhaps they missed the spectacular artwork lost in the shadows everywhere
perhaps they missed the empty road, Beckoning for drivers

we all take a moment and focus on something but as we are focused on something how can we not be aware of more

There's a Crack in the Sky

There's a crack in the sky and the light falls in between
there's a crack in the sky and it makes my life complete
there's a crack in the sky and some people will be amused
there's a crack in the sky and the world notices

I find myself questioning each and every day
why a crack in the sky is not at the forefront of the news
I find myself questioning each and every night
why a crack in the sky is not opening up the world

there's a crack in the sky and it brightened up my day
there's a crack in the sky and I felt more deeply because of it
there's a crack in the sky and it calls to us all each day
there's a crack in the sky and it fills my heart

The Way

I sometimes get lost in the moments
from the fires that burn deep within
I sometimes find myself wandering
through my mind and the pages so thin

books have been my foundation
I have read so many and more
I have stacked books by the thousands
and set them from ceiling to floor

so why is it so hard to find peace
when imagination and fire abound
and only a few fine people
has my heart ever truly found

so where is this fantastic creature
that walks as a dream within a dream
and reads with a passion as I do
and is has a ken beyond what is seen

and where are the people who see this
and understand the quest to find more
and where are the people who write it
who open up every mind's door

and I'll sit here waiting forever
for my substance will never end
looking for a fire and passion and more
and someday I know I will win

when people find truth over opinion
and stop being led to the bins
when people live for each other
and not to develop their sins

when feelings ignite our minds fury
and when we press harder to find
the depth of our love for each other
we will finally open up in our minds

I know that she is out there
surrounded by beauty and books
someone who can't be measured
except by her mind not her looks

and in the end, she will beckon me forward
and I will find my peace on that day
in the end I will know she is thither
in the end she will show me the way

Amazed

Few can understand the careful creations of such a boutique.
The light was everywhere, and I was lost in the faceted fascination before me.
Each creation unlike the previous, each hanging piece of art a testament to wonderment.
I was amazed.

I enjoyed the moments, as I looked through the glass and saw beyond.
Each magnificent careful creation a story of its own.
The easily laid shapes forming intricate excitement.
I was amazed.

I sat watching today those amazing lamps before me.
Some saw just a way to light a room, but I saw something different.
In this artistic ensemble I saw doorways into happiness.
I was amazed.

It was there that I chose a creation of blues, greens and things unseen.
I reached to it and touched face of 100 hours of work, and I knew this choice was going home with me, this choice was mine.
I was amazed.

So here I sit now with my new friend and inspiration,
Where darkness once held me captive there is light in more ways than one,
and I have found a series of stories with no end.
I am amazed.

Obscure Piece

I thought it might be worth something when I found it lying there.
Lost in a rummage sale that no one seemed to be visiting
whispering to me with its secrets that I couldn't yet hear
It was an obscure piece.

I haggled and I bartered to get this piece in front of me
why was it so important to me, it became a quest
it was the eyes, the clear solemn eyes calling to my soul
it was an obscure piece.
A price was shared and I knew I had what I wanted or did I
rushed my treasure home unsure of why I needed it so much
unsure of everything as always
It was an obscure piece.

I found myself staring, the Hazel eyes calling to me
following me everywhere that I went
I peered into those eyes and the world seemed to shimmer
It is an obscure piece.

Only the eyes existed, but I saw more now I saw the hair flowing behind her
I saw her dress dark as night slowly flapping in the wind
I continued to see and that woven Halo over her eyes widened and she seemed to move
It is an obscure piece.

what started as a spectral vision had become far more
her hand once barely visible now beckons to me, she calls me forward
her eyes glimmer as I surrender to all that she is
It is an obscure piece.

I can think of nothing but her, she caresses my mind and is painfully delicate with my soul

her gaze is upon me always and I cannot escape, I see her while I wake and while I sleep
focused or unfocused she is there and I am not sure where I end and the picture begins
It is an obscure piece.

I scream and try to get away, how long has it been? My screaming attracts neighbors and more
they rush to me trying to help but she is there, holding me tightly, writing in my thoughts
My mind reeling as others reach to me, what is this jacket they put me in, where will I go
It is an obscure piece.

As I leave, I laugh and cry as she leaves me
I am lost, gone for nevermore, she will not be there and is gone in my mind
I wonder who will take her as my things are sold in some rummage sale, and who she will take
It will be an obscure piece.

The Embrace

I felt the depth of passion
I felt as much alone
I found myself in wonder
Of all that I have known

I found the feel of darkness
and held the warmth of light
I never knew that always
Was part of day and night

I held on to the fire
and found the endless flame
I knew that I would feel this
O'er and o'er again

For when you feel the ebon
yet hold on to the light
you finally know what's true and not
and what's hidden from your sight

A new feeling

I reached down slowly to hold her face in my hands

The feelings washing over me hauntingly unfamiliar

I feel her body tense before my touch, her heart race as my hands feel her

I slowly lower my lips to touch hers

The feelings wash over me like fire across a plain

Sweeping me away in ways not easily understandable

I feel the warmth rolling across me and know

That right and wrong do not matter now

Time opens a rift and all seems to stop as we move together

Each giving no pause as we seek out our feelings

And as they open, we become more than what we were

Her Eyes

It was more than a sparkle, less than a star
it didn't really matter where I was or how far
I couldn't stop the feeling that rolled in my heart
a feeling of forever, I felt it from the start

it was more than a twinkle sprayed upon the sky
no, I didn't wonder, I saw it in her eye
I felt more than deeply, I thought it all through
I felt with such a power, it had to be true

it was more than a glimmer shining to and fro
I felt its gaze upon my bro and felt no sign of woe
I didn't want it ending I wanted it for all
I felt the feeling deeply and wanted time to stall

it outshined every flicker, bright as it could be
I felt its power rumble, deep inside of me
and when she looked upon me eyes gleaming like a sun
I knew my feelings would grow more I knew that WE had won

Happy Without Tomorrow

I sit quietly in the shadow of darkness
Surrounded by a the silence of light that only I see
And only I am a part of
Hidden from the worlds eye

She stands closely apart from me
Connected by strands we do not understand
Knowing what cannot easily be known
Yet knowing it anyway and being a part of it

Smiling we walk through the days as we can
Happy in the thought that we are out there
More than what we are alone less than what we can be
But seeing a wonderful picture today, and leaving tomorrow to tomorrow

I will be

I'm sorry you can't see me but I'll always be there
I'll be that thing that shimmers and makes other people stare
I'll be the light in morning the Crimson shards and rays
that herald and foretell the start of your new day
I'll be the rush of warmth across your gentle skin
I'll be the fuzzy feeling you get when others win
I'll be the tingle in your mind that plays upon your soul
I'll be the ring and melody that fills the aching holes
I'll love you in the morning and each and every day
I'll surround you with a feeling that will never go away
and when others see you smiling you'll know that it's true
I'll be there still watching over and always loving you

Death and Love

I brush my hands, the feel of sand falls hard.
My heart feels deep, no fire nor flame still burns.
Each mote falls free as I feel past and grieve.
I see a drop fall far, no ear can sense.
I hear a wisp that calls to depths unknown.
My soul cannot grasp light and dark abounds.
I know I feel the pain unreal or not
and when twilight shifts light to dark and nigh
my ken will breathe and come full bore once more.
She knew she was the pin that lay in stack
and she took all and cried for none and less.
Her life a shade of me and my hearts beat.
How love can pull and tug and wrench my fire
in life I felt, in death I feel now lost.

Life

I see, in mind, in heart, in soul, I know
that where I go will be a place of peace.
I see, in mind, in heart, in soul, I wish
that were I find my peace will be as I
The day is you, the day is old, so I
find my good time in fire, and fight, and more.
and when I pass the gold far light I know
I will see fire and life and keep my heart.
As I know life, and death, and all the mids
and hold each dear as none can be sans me
the dark comes fast and I find past all else
that we are all not dust but light and more
and when we know the time has come we sigh
and grasp the straws of what we know is real

The Night Goes On

It was a simple moment driving tonight
a simple moment that felt so right
I passed the car then two then three
I wasn't sure why it was me

I drove farther and faster then slower and more
I kept on driving and tried to explore
the day became night and the night was fun
for after all the night always goes on

I drove for a while and didn't feel tired
I just kept driving and I think I was wired
it wasn't a bad night nor was it good
I just kept driving because I knew that I should

and finally it came my destination was here
and not even once did I even feel fear
the day became night and the night was a song
the song kept repeating that the night goes on

I sit in my bed now about to fall asleep
I don't know whether to laugh or whether to weep
I went far and wide and hither and yon
and all the while the night goes on

The Point

I find the point inside my mind and struggle in deep throws.
I can only show the world a pathway, but not open
their minds to the depth that they could see if only they wanted to
see more than what they think is true.

I find laughter and absurdity everywhere, and it is interesting
where others can only see a little, some see more, but
in that, how can anyone see if they are not willing to look.
why is it that the sky is so blue?

I study the eyes of many and see a glimmer of hope
I know that it is there, but often the need to be right whispers they can't be wrong
and it is there we find a point, sharper that any sword
where many go, we find only a few who see

With zephyr winds and dragons fin, how can another believe
if they did not see it on CNN or FOX it must not exist
How can the world be more than a sliver of a slice of pie
How can we find the point if we cannot find a clue

Close your eyes with me once you read, see the point
it is not in towers of brick or stone, nor built in electric patterns
lost in the copper and fiber of the world, but instead the point
well, honestly, the point is within you

And knowing that will make a difference.

I Took a Journey

I sat on the precipice waiting to board
I didn't know where or when I would be found
the wishing well next to me that I could not afford
I took all that I had and more

the bus lay before me beckoning on
I wanted to be there, I wanted to move forward
if only I entered then I would be gone
I took all that I had and more

so starts a journey, a wish from a coin
the Taco Bell beckoned, the moments ground on
the others not like me I would soon join
I took all that I had and more

another step forward, never a step back
known and unknown, a well of forgotten dreams
I carried nothing, I need not have packed
I took all that I had and more

a journey of wonder, a journey of light
the pain and the power and more came to me
each day battle, each day a fight
I took all that I had and more

I'll find a way now, I'll find every path
never to stop to overcome it all
I will keep striving, I will still laugh
I took all that I had and more

You can come with me, reach out your hand
find your inner power, let go of all
Take a deep breath, and you will understand
you have all that you need and more

WooHoo

She is my morning
She is my night
I love and cheer
with forever light

I smile in early
and when I sleep
and find in patience
her heart to keep

Feathers and Scales

Feathers and scales are thought of at night
as children of men decide the wrong and the right
Yama calls Karma and decides some fate
and people consider the power to wait

Life and death are Easter's great lessons
Where moments of pain gave eternal blessings
and fury nor fate can forget at all
If Dante had not called to open the wall

If Nick can know when he must bring coal
how can we all just write like a fool
How can we know the words of Themis
when we can't see beyond the things as they seem

Why must we wait for judgement to come
Why must we teach the old and not young
How can we better our lives and our selves
So in our happiness we all might delve

Trust in the thought that all are as should
and you give an excuse for the bad, not the good
Instead find the courage to rise far above
and when darkness descends you will conquer with love

A moment not taken a day without end
My goodness and feelings I often will send
As when we started, as when it's done
Keep good in your heart and you will have won

Awe

I find myself in awe again lost in the moments
as people grasp for words and ideas and I look upon it all
it is not the picture were the premise that inspires what I write
but the people, the people that see beyond the picture, and don't live by the rules before them

I find myself in awe again paying attention to it all
personalities abound and I am mesmerized by many who are more talented than they know
I find myself enjoying the words and phrases that come to my mind
I find myself honoring those who would overcome to achieve

I find myself in awe again paying attention to the picture
I am lost in a geometric moment anchored to the earth
I easily imagine swimming between pious pylons
and wonder how connected we all are

I find myself in awe at the convergence
there it is, some of us close, some far away
as I squint my eyes the pictures become one and the people are as the pylons
some tight and close taking chances and some farther away holding and doing still

I find myself in awe of it all
there will come a day when I will understand
there will come a day when others will see it too
but still the waves of life lap at us all

I find myself in awe of an art
that finds a way to see the words that others miss
and somehow build a picture from very little
and it is there that vision and emotion become one

I find myself in awe

and it is there that I should be
when I am no longer awed by life
it is time to go away

Find yourself in awe
be fiery in this world each moment
be the force of nature always
and let your words guide the way

Walking Wild

a deep breath
a slow thrum
a tiny move
I find my way

a huge sigh
another step
shuffle forward
the path is there

a slight cough
stumble on
feel it all
just keep going

another lungful
another foot
it might hurt
but you can't let it

exhale again
feel the burn
it's not far
another milestone

It's about you

The sun shines and the bird sings
 life goes on and I enjoy the moment
 the wind blows and the trees wave
 cars drive by and I count them one by one
 the waves crash and the fish swim
 boats saunter along and I revel in the ripples
 time flies and the moments pass
 the clock hands turn and time can't last
 the rock sits and never moves
 beneath it all life happens
 the sun shines and the days go on
 time stands still and I still enjoy the moment

Look away...

I watch
 a victim of the gorgons long before most were born
 feeling each day, hurt and forlorn
 understanding all around me but there is nothing I can do

Eyes up
 I scan the sky looking for peace
 I find very little, minds never at ease
 if only they could hear my cries, and know what I could have brought to them

Chin up
 I have no choice, but to slowly decay
 forgotten, and dissolving away from it all
 thousands of years and you still are the same

Don't
 get lost in the negativity that is so easy to grasp
 beheld away from the positivity
 keep staring when what you see is not what you need

Breathe deep
 the world is full of positives if you look for them
 let go the negatives and see beyond
 turn away before you suffer as I have

Find your way
 stop letting others tell you where to go|
 stop being just another follower
 choose the path that will find your happiness

Intertwine
 the world is yours if you want it
 be a leader of yourself, let others follow, or not
 find the right way for you

I was
fascinated by the gorgon
staring at the negativity and hating it
unable to look away until I was frozen for all time

I know
thousands of years looking at you all
unable to tell you that I would be with you
if I had only looked away

Another Day

Another day of laughing, another day to cry
I find myself wondering, if another day I'll find
I push myself and forward is a direction I will go
I strive to learn more every day but how little do I know

I found myself in good times, I knew myself in bad
and every day I found that life was the best I ever had
I reached out every morning and squeezed the world so tight
and somehow deep inside myself I always found the light

Yet somewhere in the morning and somewhere in the night
I found myself straining for things just out of sight
after all was said and done and I could see no more
I pushed myself again to find the farthest shore

I knew that I had saw it, and I knew that it was true
but somewhere deep inside me I had to find a clue
the moments were fantastic the memories even more
and I will just keep pushing to find that farther shore

Purely Passionate Purpose

Once Upon a time
that's all you need to say
Once Upon a time

As the day opened and new challenges arise
as the sun rises and the world becomes a bigger place
as clouds form from a thousand thousand imperfections
beauty is born

If I am imperfect, and I beautiful?
Can I feel the sound within my heart?
Does my drive make me driven?
Can my passion find a limit?

Pure and powerful forevermore
Never lost and never found
Pushing forward always
I will find a way

Once Upon a time
that's all you need to say
Once Upon a time
My story is forever

What is it?

I often get lost in a thought
it's bitter and seems to sting
and I find myself in mourning

I often find my heart right there
I never realized how important it is
to hear every single beat

I often see things others fail to see
and wonder why I need glasses
when my eyes don't even need to open

I often think of other worlds
but in the midst of it all I wonder
and somewhere there is more

I often think of you
and I don't even know you or your name
and we laugh together without ever having met

I find a hole in the sky
and put my heart in it
because underneath it all I'm still here

I often wonder about
nothing in particular, just about
and all of the possibilities that might be

I Missed You

I missed you before I met you
I felt it each and every day
I saw you in the shadows
and in the light that came my way

I missed you before I met you
and the feelings deep inside
called to me every morning
and I didn't know even why

I felt you as my heartbeat
I saw you in my sleep
I didn't know what you looked like
or the time that we would keep

our time together forever
but gone in just a blink
the things that I'd been feeling
were thoughts that I could think

I missed you before I met you
I met you and lived so strong
the depth of every moment
it was almost like a song

it hurts sometimes to think of
pain greater then I know
if I missed you before I met you
then why did you have to go?

Broken Science

I found myself listening to someone about science
they talked about the finite wonderment of knowing
and as they did I realized they knew nothing about science
and instead knew how to listen to someone else

there is a poetic nature to science because it's not part of what is and it's not part of what isn't. Science is how we defined what we think we prove until we can't prove it anymore. Then it becomes science again, like a dream within a dream within reality.

 Who would have thought that lightning could be trapped in a copper strand. Was it magic or science? Before or after it became science did it change? Always changing, always lost in itself, always growing beyond itself. Who makes up this line that builds science?

 and here I sit, knowing science is there, but also realizing that science both is and is not. If science is finite then why keep learning, if science is infinite, then why say science is a rule? Science is as much magic as magic is science. Can you not see past yourself?

I paused for a moment

I spent time looking at a pristine beach only to see what was behind
people cried and people laughed but mostly people laughed and enjoyed what they wanted to see
behind them the cooling towers and storage tanks created a synergistic nightmare
heaven and hell combined, technology and nature fusing as one

there can be no moments where our world is not encroaching upon what was
but the talented among us find a way to see the beauty in it all
dinosaurs lasted for so long and we are less than a blip of a blip on the face of this planet
people worry people are sad thinking the planet will end, it did not when they were gone

the only thing that will end is perhaps us
lost in our arrogance that we can eliminate a world
I smile upon the face of the beach and enjoy what I have from all that I see
take away one and I would be sad, take away both and I would be far sadder

we cannot exist without nature, most are not equipped to exist without technology
to give up technology would eliminate us far more effectively than global warming
no posts to make, nor microwave dinners, as many cradle long dead phones and join them
a bitter end, lost in chaos, taking the breath from us all

so I look out upon the seen before me and except the beauty of the beach
I enjoy the waves against my feet and feel the breeze waft across my face
and I enjoy the rust finding its way upon the bare metals built by

man
and know that the power it creates allow so many to live

still before me is another day and perhaps I will smile and laugh
as nuclear waves make their way across the world
for in the end the world will survive and find a way with or without us
and someday the beauty will be born again, even if I won't be there

Incessant

A picture there in my mind
cluttered, forceful, lost in a mulch of other thoughts
A child, lost in my thoughts, but forever at the forefront

It is not as so many reassured
pain, sorrow, and pure agony assails me
A child, crying in the night, silent as I search for them

I am lost in the center of my soul
form, fury, the anger is real and apparent
A child, shallow in the well of infinite tears

I cannot let go of the real
grief, despair, the darkness that I must overcome
A child, torn memories, no more rings to reach

Why and wherefore
hope, time, and the love we shared
A child, life is too short, even when it's not

A future of reflection
precious, remnant, holding on to what is positive
A child, gone forever, in my mind infinitely incessant

A world may know
always, everyone, most can understand
A child, never forgotten, never to be found

Look away...

I watch
 a victim of the gorgons long before most were born
 feeling each day, hurt and forlorn
 understanding all around me but there is nothing I can do

eyes up
 I scan the sky looking for peace
 I find very little, minds never at ease
 if only they could hear my cries, and know what I could have brought to them

chin up
 I have no choice, but to slowly decay
 forgotten, and dissolving away from it all
 thousands of years and you still are the same

don't
 get lost in the negativity that is so easy to grasp
 beheld away from the positivity
 keep staring when what you see is not what you need

breathe deep
 the world is full of positives if you look for them
 let go the negatives and see beyond
 turn away before you suffer as I have

Find your way
 stop letting others tell you where to go|
 stop being just another follower
 choose the path that will find your happiness

Intertwine
 the world is yours if you want it
 be a leader of yourself, let others follow or not
 find the right way for you

I was
 fascinated by the gorgon
 staring at the negativity and hating it
 unable to look away until I was frozen for all time

I know
 thousands of years looking at you all
 unable to tell you that I would be with you
 if I had only looked away

Justice

I lost myself in the light of fear
and found nowhere to go
I wound myself in the coils I wear
of terror, thrills, and woe

The dragons breath was upon my heart
as if I felt alive
and I felt the crisp air the tore life apart
and knew that I would strive

The scales of justice were lost again
and I held my head in shame
For people fall and become insane
and who then is to blame

I felt the world fall down on me
as I rose to a vile task
Who would do it and I would see
but Charon dared to ask

A thousand bones in a string of pearls
were part of early calls
filled with young and old and poor and earls
The light the shine of old

The time has come as new bones fill
my never-ending function
the fear of death and Charon's will
has drove us to this junction

I lost myself in the light of fear
and now I see my path
I will walk on and not shed a tear
until my job is past

as final moment comes, and I complete his task
I lay back down to sleep, awaiting my next ask

Tearcicles

A strong wind blows the tears from my eyes
I'm not sure where they came from
I wipe my cheeks as they turn to ice
and I wonder why I am where I am

the wind whips past as the snow sticks to my face
I blink my eyes in disbelief at the irony
is it the wind or the snow or something else
allusion and illusion find their way deep inside my heart

I closed my eyes and I'm lost in the maelstrom
is it the sky that reflects upon me or me that reflects upon the sky
I watch ice crystals fall from my face
I wonder just how deep the cuts are

visions stands across my eyelids
of a past with a future
now I have a future without that past
the wind takes my breath away

all I ever wanted was all I ever gave
no quarter given and just right without a chore
if only a moment could be a little more
I bow my head and feel the breeze grind to a halt

Just for Me

I'd like to think I know myself
better than anyone else
I'd like to think I see the world
without just time to kill

I'd like to think I'm happy too
without worry rhyme or care
I'd like to think the world is ours
no matter how we fare

I'd like to think I'll be around
to enjoy the things I like
but often I get lost in thought
as days pass in to night

I'd like to think that happiness
this is something we all crave
but I know I may be blind
or perhaps a little naïve

I'd like to think I know myself
and yes, I think I do
I'll be happy with just that for now
and I know that I'll be true

Shadows of Passion

I
If
Ink
Love
Hours
Spirits
Entwined
Shelter
Seeker
Feels
Fire
She
Hi
U

Bitter Passion

It starts as a longing, a need, a want combined
One asks of its alright, another says fine
The lines they are drawn, with haphazard care
and no one can see them, for they are not there

A time for reflection, for power and lust
A time for betrayal, and unnerving trust
It builds up inside each, pulling and pulled
Forever it holds us, while changing its mold

The sky is the limit, or so they say
but no man can keep it, no matter that way
The fire shifts slightly, and pulls to and fro
and which way will hold us, no one can know

Whether woman or man, or some other fire
One comes back to us, if any retire
No worries or cares, or anything given
The plasma burns brightly a flame never ending

Why walk the path of passion, because it is enough
Why walk the path of passion, when it can be of so tough
Make every day a mission, to find passion good or bitter
and never let your passion ebb, and never be a quitter

Timberfall

Awkward angles cover my field of vision
The scattered anti-parallel lines also cover my field
I love my trees and watch them grow
but in the wind I watch them fall and die

They rock back and forth
The wind plays games with the limbs
over and over the trees strains to survive
but the wind knows no limit or bound

It is said if a tree falls in the forest, does it make a sound
Does it scream in pain as the wind rends root and bark
Does it feel the loneliness of a stranded traveller
If a tree falls is it remembered should it be art

I swing my axe to remove the tree
Or work the saw to cut it to my needs
Is it still a tree? Who decided when a tree becomes wood?
Why? Grass shavings are still grass.

A field without trees is a dustbowl
A garden is a place to grow more than trees
but why did we decide that a tree was less important
Or is that why we made it wood?

For now, I will enjoy my wood and my trees
and clear the old, and plant anew
and somewhere, a tree will sigh in the wind
as another one becomes a rocking chair

And there we will rock in the wind

That Moment

Here I am in that moment again.
It is familiar but foreign as I wonder what will happen in the seconds that follow. The understanding that I am not truly in control of what is next. Understanding that I may assert control even as control is being asserted on me.

Here I am in that moment again.
Memories and more flood my mind as I am forced to consider time as an abstract, defined but not definable, fluid yet rigid, and I know I will not feel more that I feel, or less than What I have felt. I am aware of the unending paths lain before me.

Here I am in that moment again.
Constantly aware of what and where and how yet never why. That question seems to evade and perplex, what is the why of it, is there a means to an end or am I that means to an end. Is there even a possibility that an end can be defined?

Here I am in that moment again.
Once again with precise clarity, knowing the possibilities and the impossible. Aware there is more than my cognizance allows. I am challenged by it all as I grapple for a solution that will end this bout with providence. I believe in me.

Here I am in that moment again.
Past, illusionary control again is restored. I know it is an artifice born of mortal desperation, but I have cavorted with the keepers far too often and know the control is there. Another last gleaming passes and I have learned more for the next time.

Breathe Deep

Breathe deep they said and didn't see that I already drew
a breath of life from everywhere and never had a clue

A breath in time saves many, and more breaths even more
and as I breathe I know that all the world is for sure

Struggle to stay breathing, for that is the depth of life
and even if it's harder, fight on no matter strife

As morning turns to evening, and evening turns to night
breathe deep the depth of all that is, and never fail the fight

Understood a little...

I find myself in unfamiliar ground
a lot transpires and the light continues
I see people come and go
each with a perspective all their own
each with a message to carry forward

there is little I can do and even less to show
in a world full of places that exist only in a dream
I was there at the start and I knew where it would go
but no one sees except those who look
and no one looks until they see

so where does this world of bits and bytes lead us
except to a conclusion that we couldn't understand
and a piece of peace that may never come
as another moment scrolls by
and blue light blots the horizon

it won't be Jabberwock nor eat or drink
it won't be a moment with what we think
instead the world will close in on us
and in the end only the shadow will remain
and the long lost comment that no one read

I wish I hadn't seen it coming
but I knew the shallow would be easier
and that love and lust and hate and hatred are fine
if no threat is given for being real
in the end we should all understand

Already

It was January already when I saw the light

and February when I made it right

March came and went, and I laughed and smiled

And April was there for just a little while

May came and went like a spring shower

and June made me laugh for another hour

Then July was a fun and wild ride

as August slipped in by my side

September called forth the stormy skies

but October never made me ask why

November gave us turkeys and to fight

then December brought on the longer night

I made it through another year's trials

I know I will be fine for a little while

and when in life I must be stronger

I wish life was a little longer

Row?

Play play play your heart
madly through the scenes
angrily angrily angrily angrily your peace may be a dream

Driven

Driven in the moment, passion takes the lead
Driven to go faster, a quiet need for speed
Driven in the daytime, driven in the night
Driven so we get there, across the gilded light

We find our way to get here
We find our way to more
We can find a moments respite
and the we drive some more

When tiresome moments come here
and lose us in the eve
we once again go faster
and find tremendous speed

Driven in the morning
We get there every day
I keep driving often
and I will find my way.

Posted Life

I feel a life that stretches on and never seems to end, the life I want, the life I need, a life I can depend. No not a diaper, instead a life that people may find true, a deeper life, a longer life, a life that I make true. A life that stretches on and on, can be a special bond, but I will find the different way, a way I'll always find. With zephyr winds that blow on high, and people that help the world, I'll go around and round and round and take life for a whirl. Another day, another dime, another way to see, I'll find myself another way, and still, I will be me. To thine self you must be true, and heed my easy words, the world is yours if you want it to be, a life with uncrossed swords. Again, I say that you be you, to that you must adhere, and as you walk through another day, set aside your fear and just live.

The Mountain

one more mountain, one more climb

one more moment in search of rhyme

A see the base and shudder twice

for who would want another fight

The day is young and my knees are strong

and I will push to get along

The mid of day is coming fast

I pray my heart will always last

One more step and I push on hard

What was the thing I'm going toward?

A rock slides back and I take a fall

Is it going to be worth it all

Another jump and I still push on

once brown hair now gray or gone

I feel the challenge in my mind

and hold on for this thing called time

The top is close and so many failed

the winds howl forth and wolve still wail

and as I reach the summits crest

I know that I have done my best

Time is slow and time is fast

Nothing easy ever lasts

The depth of power upon my brow

Nothing defining then and now

Again I find myself at the base

of mountain high and find my pace

for one thing down another rose

and a life of mountains is what I chose

Angrily

Play play play your heart
madly through the scenes
angirly angrily angrily angrily your peace may be a dream

Time for a Nap

Another day, another night, time just slips away
another word, flying free, not sure what to say
I ask why, no answer comes, will it ever change
adapt again, not my choice, my life to rearrange

another day, another mourn, another lost advantage
another whisper, thunders down, my choice means no rage
I shake my head, but I won't show, the feelings that I feel
and every moment, deep inside, I know that I should heal

life is fair, all you do, is make the world happen
another moment, time is lost, my choice and my outcome
whether chore or no, whether deepest night, I tire of the game
no matter what I say, or what I do, the outcome is the same

another day, another month, the years go on and on
another time, another place, until we all are gone
the moments come, the moments go, they'll never see the gap
today is mine, I'll fight it all, and then I'll take a nap

Awake Now

and here I lie awake now
while others lie and sleep
I haven't said my prayers yet
nor held my soul to keep

the morning comes eventual
the night stays far too long
and here I lie alone now
not sure of verse or song

my time is all before me
I live it everyday
and as you fall to sleep again
I won't get in the way

a million other moments
or perhaps a million more
what lies before me
is what I have in store

for when you wake in morning
from silence ohh so deep
I just want you to know
I lie awake as you sleep

Battle

A simple shop a friendly witch
No reason why no soul to stitch
No worry or cry, the moments last
The world is better, the spell is cast

An evil beast with fervent goals
A fire within him creates hot coals
No quarter given, he strives to take
A life not given that death foresakes

The foulest deed to comprehend
A soul of evil now descends
Bitter fate is not yet done
As evil fights but has not yet one

The friendly witch now glows asunder
The evil ghoul is made to wonder
With blinding light and fiery scorn
The battle raged like brazen storm

As the witch began to fall
The world shuttered with her call
Then plant and animal stood and grew
and friendly witch stood with life anew

Evil comes and evil goes
And in a battle they should know
This witches world they cannot breach
From witch who holds our souls to teach

Evil thought that they would win
and hold our lives in evil sin
but now evil sits encased in glass
to sell to other witches caste

The potion here, a spell sits there
On shelves aligned with chilly air

Evil came and tried to win
and built the stock and store within

A simple shop a friendly witch
No reason why no soul to stitch
No worry or cry, the moments last
The world is better, the spell is cast

Across a Universe

I find myself in numbers, and lost in abject awe
For how can we know anything, when seasons rise and fall
For some it was the ancients, and people long since gone
Others think of long ago, and the feelings that we long

We shuffle through the morning, and slither through the night
We stand out in the open, or hide from other's sight
We spread our wings and fly some, and break the surly bonds
or hide in near dark forests, between the healthy fronds

The question that comes easy, is are we now alone
The sky can set us thinking, and wondering about our home
We feel the dread of winter, and enjoy the summer days
but life can sometimes task us, as we try to find our ways

So how then can I find you, another kindred soul
How can I find peace now, with silence as a goal
Where can it be starting, and where will it soon end
and when can I reach out now, to one that I call friend

I see you when I'm sleeping, and when my mind just drifts
I know that you are there still, not lost in winsome drifts
and when we smile and laugh soon, the bitterness with end
across all time and space now, you will always be my friend

The White Tower

What purpose could there be for near infinite wisdom in one place?
Here where the writings on the wall are a wall that spans forever?
Was the design from the lines of a swan or the curves of an angels face
Who thought this masterpiece was a worthwhile endeavor

there is much I could enjoy in every moment in the depths of this monument
that defines our greatest achievement, the words that flow from our being
it doesn't matter to which section I would be sent
what matters is the memories I would find in between

while others listen to opinions played on a zero
this tower of white purpose defines a different approach
where angry words don't invade our minds and make liars heroes
where our decisions create a knowledge where none can encroach

No book denied, no thought left behind, instead of sides we can see all sides
and realize that inside of the truth are many truths, expressed without bias
in these moments I hope minds stay wide and set aside the opinion guides
and on wings of fire and ice our minds can finally fly us

when one book is done there is another, and another moment to learn
another page, another volume, we will find our way
and at the end of all that is, perhaps we will create another page to turn
and there perhaps one day we will guide the way

How many sunsets?

One moment is upon us
Another will come up soon
The time to act is coming
 and not to sing another tune

Another day is here now
Where did the others go
The time slips like an oyster
as it comes it will soon go

I find myself in heaven
or is this really hell?
I feel the world pass by me
and wonder if I fell

The skies they light the shadows
and time keeps going still
I'm not sure what the moment is
but soon I know I will

How many sunsets coming?
How many will I see?
How many times for all to know
that my soul will be so free

I fought the moments early
and when my days were young
I found a life before me
and behind the world sung

There is no time set for us
no set time for us all to live
no one knows when it will come
so every day let's live

Collapsible

Some say the world is a giant place
others say that it is very small
I'm not sure why I care a little
because I am very very tall

some say days are too long
others say days are just right
I think days are what they are
I just am tired of their fight

My fight's inside and walks along
and other think I am not sure
but I know that inside my heart
lies the answer, the only cure

The world is ripe and people see
the motion and matter that is me
and only one heart can truly be true
and that heart is always true

and small still I find the world
while other shrink I grow still
will giant leaps and calming bows
I collapse the world to my will

At the Core

Passion. Silent Specter of the night. They who take me towards the light. Forever wandering yet out of sight.

Feeling. Deeply lost in transparent arms. Tingles, reaching, out of harm. Holding hearts and keeping warm.

Forever. More than dreams can pull away. Real as thunder, night, and day. No, my heart will never sway.

Tomorrow. Another day is here and now. I saw their eyes and felt the wow. Into my heart the here and now. Is this love?

Check It Out

The world goes round and round and I feel the darkness

around the ragged rock it ran and the darkness feels me

There is a side to everyone that stands above

and it is the light that I will be sure to see

as darkness flows upon this land and i see it rise

I can only consider the depths of the light in me

for others can strive to fight or join

I will reach inside and dispel the dark i see

For what price can we reach for, to quell the dark of night

and what will be do to make the world afire and see it through

as others ebb and flow, I will find the feelings I need

and those may well be of you

Colors

Mara the dreamer gave us colors unreal and sealed the edge of our fate

Well Brahma spoke loudly and gave us the world so that we wouldn't have to wait

God made the world in only six days and Jehovah they say did it too

The tomes all confirm it and make it all real so we know that this must be the truth

And Cronus gave time to a place in our space so that chaos in order would bend

But Zeus overcame him and created a world where his works likely would never end

Gitche Manitou spoke in the world became something it hadn't been before

The fabric of all was upon us again and humanity might never fall

Again and again the colors unreal made us wonder the edge of our fate

Three sisters cut thread and we understand that as people we cannot just wait

Days are before us and days are behind and in the process we fight through it all

Our life everlasting with limits upon us and time doesn't matter at all

So fight for the normal, fight for the right and do it without question or pause

Because whatever happened, whatever's been, we must fight for a heavenly cause

Touch

Soft as a butterfly's wings

Hot as a fiery ember

Hard as the armor of a tank

Slippery as oiled ice

How do we know and how do we feel, touch and wonder are all that is real, telling another what we're going through, hearts torn asunder hearts born anew

Painful as mercurochrome

Fuzzy has a bunny

Smooth as glass

Rough as a cat's tongue

It's easy to see what another must know, all we must do is understand and show, let's feel all around us and tell them just how, let's let them understand us and understand now

99

99 minutes an hour 28 hours a day

My life is full of the power, the power that I need to play

88 seconds a minute, 500 days a year

I find a way to overcome everything, and set aside all my fear

Forever and ever I think this, forever and more I think that

Forever is never enough now, forever is right where it's at

I thank you for spending your time now, I thank you for spending with me

And if you don't think the same now, Open your mind and be free

Rolling

I hear the thunder rolling

I see the thunder crash

While others they just listen

I hear the thunder smash

What others see as truth now

What others want to see

The thunder doesn't care

The thunder moves to me

You think you know the answer

I think I never do

I have to listen closely

To find out what is true

The thunder doesn't care

And the lightning sends it high

While everyone else sees the thunder

I'm just asking why

Drain

I'd like to think that drains go down
and filter out the rest
I like to think that drains are good
and make the world seem best

but drains are swirling mists of muck
and often we just want to scream "oh yuck"
and people are tired of losing luck
and want to just say "what the ..."

I'd like to think that drains go down
and filter out the rest
and if I work to make it so
perhaps not like the rest

and drains are hollow and need to clean
awhile people shallow, are often mean
and why is life never as it seems
it just makes me want to scream
and still, at the end of the day, it is a good day

AI

A microbe ran the gambit across the setting sky
A fish became a walker
Or the sun spread out the sky
We think we know "what's up doc"
and yet the world stands firm
that AI is the answer
or AI should be spurned

but do we know the answer
of when it first came time
do we know the answer
of who will learn to rhyme
we see AI as hated
but I know that its true
a next gen of AI slaves now
Is that what we want to do?

Reasons

I'd like to think the reason why is a reason that I need to try
I'd like to think the world is old, so I can do as someone told
I'd like to think the world so clear is never ever full of fear
I'd like to think the endless night is a place of wonder and not of fright
I'd like to think I am full of peace, so my mind can find its deep relief
I'd like to think, and think some more, because that is what we are here for

Beyond

There is a pain
I felt it today, it had its way, it took me away
I know it is bad, I can't think nor be sad, it makes me mad
The depth of it all, whether great or small, not worth the fall

I feel it too deep
Coursing through life, it cuts like a knife, is this truly life
Sighing I turn, I feel my legs burn, my stomach it churns
Why was it me, from pain I am free, Can I not see

Control once again
The hurt is still there, from toes to my hair, and I am aware
No pain is a choice, I have a voice, no need to make noise
The cost is my peace, but it brings relief, yes pain is a thief

What cost

I feel the deep pain
it rips my soul asunder
Never surrender

Undone

What is it in a child's laugh that opens hearts
and brings out the joy in the world for only a moment

How deep is a word of thanks brings a smile
and relieves the weight of the world upon us

How kind is a word of hope
The gives us all a way to see far more than we thought

How wonderful to see anger undone
and a world that can see beyond the piece of reality unseen

Spree

Another moment cherished, another moment gone, I fill my cart too quickly, and then I will be gone
A cart filled with the little, and even with the big, a cart that can't be seen by most, no matter what they think
I find myself still shopping, a little with my cart, I know the day is waning, but when will evening start?

A time in the middle

A time in the middle
Nowhere to see
A time to make sound
A time to just see
A time in the highlands
A time in the low
A time to move fast
A time to move slow
A time to be quiet
A time to be loud
A time to be humble
A time to be proud
A time to wake up
A time that we keep
A time no to laydown
A time to go sleep

Strong

There's strong and then stronger and stronger than that
There's playing with rocks and lifting the cat
A little boys dream and a lifelong with
Be as strong as you can, and swim like a fish

Why

A big ole problem
Never wanting to be found
A wise solution

Sweet

I find the world to be so sweet
nothing else just complete

a moment passed and nothing more
while I struggle and reach the door

the days are long and never more
will I find what I'm looking for

I'll stand and face the hounds of hell
but no one knows what I know will

and when the day is once complete
I know I'll never know defeat

succeed or fail there is no issue
we'll find it all and it will be true

Dark sounds

The sleek sound of dark
Seriousness is aside
why is it so quiet

Paradox

A slide to the left, a pace to the right
The world turns and I find my fight
I work so hard and shine so bright
That darkness may never hold the night

And when the world seems asleep
I pray to all my soul to keep
No good nor bad nor ever sheep
and forever strong but able to weep

Whosoever can be found
and holds the soul for getting down
can find their day is now unwound
a thunderous silence full of sound

I'll stand and fight to make the peace
and wear the coat when it should be fleece
then by the home that I should lease
and hold on tight and turn the keys

Timeless

Some think time is finite
and yes that is quite true
I think time has limits
and most will say to too

and when it goes far and farther
and when it can run out
then time will just be timeless
until another bout

Be full of time my friend now
and make the world complete
and as we find more time now
we will never face defeat

Why ask why?

Kinda like a story
that maybe can come true
we find a lot of worries
asking why to me and you

But Clown made us remember
that why is never good
and how is a better question
and layer the fun as it should

So set aside your why now
and make the world complete
cuz how is so much fun to see
and we will skip defeat

Higher

Fly higher
Open you mind to more and more
Reach to the sky without hands

Be you
Open your heart to feel deeply
Reach out with your heart

See farther
Find the depth of an ocean
Or the length of the eternal sky

Clumps

I often find myself in a bit of a clump
I'm not sure about why
I often go there and often jump
but I know that I will try

we find ourselves on hallowed ground
without worry cry or care
we find ourselves in another clump
and are not sure how we'll fare

a clump of this a clump of that
it never seems to end
while others push to not get fat
the clumpy is here again

I think I like the clumpy times
because I think it's true
that I'd rather really be clumpy
than ever have to be blue

Leverage

Seriously?
A task so daunting it cannot be done
A world around that seems unbound
A fire inside that pushes for one
Solutions so strange it seems like fun

Lifting pulling, pushing hard
Neither way allows a shard
no quarter given by foot or yard
push the street or boulevard

Finally done by Archimedes rule
The edge of all can be a tool
we find a way for we are not a fool
and work so hard just like a mule

Spoons

Forkin spoons the knife would say
and put the silverware away
and soon it withers but rarely gone
A steel for one and ne'er gone wrong

With masterful might I find a way
I push and pull and down they lay
To spoon and hold the day so dear
nor sound or moment that we hear

A fork again has come to time
with every single counter tine
and when the fork is done and gone
we all will feel that we have won

Silence

Silence is golden
I may want silver
Silence that I am holding
for the reason

Why so silent
it is in my head
I find that I went
So far and then

I found the feeling
that I missed
My mind was reeling
and I was lost

If on this time we would be wed
I miss the quiet in my head
The sound of silence is now dead
all because so are you

Not quite the stars

A day before me
I found myself in my own mind
Lost in the depth of what you know as time

A day to be
I am what I can be in the moment
and without that won't say I can't

Tomorrow comes
None too soon, but not too long
My mind sings a happy song

Wish

The future is always nonsense until it becomes the past
Things that mean the most always seem to last

I feel the body electric absorb my ways
but I know not how the world plays

Until the end we screech and shout
and we only know what we know about

And then the world come into our hearts
and leaves a plethora of little shards

Pluralized

Another day upon the world and we stand wondering
Why is it that so many days pass and go further
and in the end we find a deep chasm
and find ourself seeing into the abyss of the past
yet now, does it truly make a difference?

Foci

What is the focus of the world?
Where do we begin and where does everyone else end?
Why do we ask dumb questions?
Why does a fish swim?

Why in the world do we look the wrong way
never thinking right from wrong.
Why in the world do we let our minds play
until the right idea comes along?

Where in the world is our life now?
What in the world can it be?
How will we learn to focus
when we can't even learn how to see?

When will we know it's all over
when we finally see the world pass?
How will we know what our life is
when we're all too afraid just to ask?

Focus on things that you love
and ask the right questions each day
and then when someone asks how you focus
show them what you have to say.

Inside

I find myself lost inside my mind
I always am finding a way out but it is deep and long
it is filled with the things that I am and that I am not
it is filled with much, much more
I sit and ponder the secrets of the universe
and realize that I only know a fraction of a fraction of what the universe is
I consider what I know and realize there is only a small amount that calls to me
so many limits on the inside, so many limits on the outside
I see others struggle with the same
some of them know their limits and some of them surely do not
and in the end the biggest lesson is
don't call me Shirley

Footnotes and Follies

I Took a Journey

This was a very unique poem. It was based on a picture however I found it to be a little more enlightening than many of my compatriots.

The picture was quite stunning and opened up a greyhound bus and a wishing well and a few other things that looked pretty cool. I laughed about it and the poem took a life of its own. I considered the journeys that we've all been on and thought about how the world sees these journeys. I thought about how people sometimes find the adventure and things and other times miss the magical moments they could have. As I finished this poem I laughed because I used a unique rhyming scheme and a fairly unique structure, but most of all I found that it fit. I hope you take a deep breath and understand how I came to it.

It's about you

It may be hard to believe but I get a lot of interaction with my readers. Sometimes it's very direct and sometimes it's more passive. One of the most common questions I get is them asking if my poem or post was about them.

It's funny how that happens. Lots of people are going through a lot of things and occasionally they overlap. Sometimes more than others. There are also things that go on that are common in our everyday and we can find some thought in it without really trying.

In this poem there are a series of unrelated events that are all interconnected. I wrote this from first person but it can easily fall into third person without even thinking about it. What got me were the layers when I was writing it. Saying the sun shines and the bird sings could be a simple statement but it can also define a season or a time or a state of mind. Are we the bird? Where is the sun shining? Is it shining on us?

A common theme in many of my discussions is time and often as I discussed time it flies by. In this particular poem I set the stage by looking at a rock that isn't even there. I hope you can take a breath and pay attention to what's happening below the surface and not just on top of it.

I Missed You

I pretty much got lost in this one night for no apparent reason. Several people who have read my poetry have talked about pain and all the pain that I must have felt. They go to a particular poem, and pull out a few lines, then explain to me how bad I hurt. I don't agree or disagree, I just know that I needed to write.

As I wrote this particular poem I found myself lost in a circle thinking about the past, the present, and the future. It's a place I don't really like to be simply because the future hasn't happened yet in the past only helped get me where I am. The place that I need to go was somewhere in the present, defining myself and my day. With that in mind, somewhere there was someone who wanted to be there with me for more than just there simple and complex needs, who instead wanted an adventure with me.

Don't we all think about that sometimes? Don't we look at the world that we have and wonder if someone could actually see who we were and open things up to the next level, and maybe a little more.

Inside

Ever have one of those days where you are inside your mind trying to figure out how you got there? At the essence of inside is the idea that we challenge our own minds and challenge ourselves consistently. Of course I had to throw in a little humor, but sometimes we just don't get how much of an impact we have upon ourselves.

Leverage

I sat listening to myself one day and all of the things that I was fighting against. There are challenges that each of us face and sometimes we don't know how to handle those challenges. Sometimes we do. For me I continue to pound on a challenge until I overcome it, and as I spent time on this day and on this poem I realized that all you need is a longer lever to move the world. Yes I know, it's not always that easy. But I would like to suggest by poem that perhaps it's just a matter of seeing things a different way and pushing a little harder.

Sunsets

Those who know me know that I write at 29,000 sunsets each day. It is a blog site I have kept up for almost 10 years. As I sit patiently and watch the sunset I often think about how finite the universe is and how much we need to pay attention to what is going on.

At the core of it all is what I consistently stayed at 29,000 sunsets. If we only had a finite number of days and knew that tomorrow would be our last, what would we do different. Why aren't we doing it now

About the Author

Andrew Allen Smith was born in Anderson, Indiana. Until the age of fifteen, he moved at least once per year and finally settled in Lexington, Kentucky. Andrew spent a significant amount of his teenage years reading and writing short stories, attempts at novels, and poetry. He published his first book, "A Slice of Passion," in 2005. It was a book of poetry compiled from dozens of years of work.

In 2015, Andrew published "The Theft and Other Short Stories" as a collection of some of his favorite portions of his writings after he was challenged to self-publish a book. Challenged and excited about his success, he published his first novel, "Vengeful Son," in 2016 and began building a franchise with that book. "The Masterson Files" (the series containing "Vengeful Son") now includes five books and has fifteen in outline form. The story follows an ex-assassin that is reluctantly engaged in helping others while trying to retire.

In 2020, after a tragic event, Andrew co-wrote "What NOT to Say to People Who Are Grieving." This book showcased emotions and an approach to helping others be more mindful of their words during grief. HE is currently working on a follow up to that book, "How NOT to Grieve".

2021 gave us "A Slice of Fear" followed by "Another Slice of Fear" with short stories focusing on fears of all types. "Another Slice of Fear" won Andrew a Literary Titan Award and has been reviewed positively for several stories in the genre. This was followed in 2022 with "Yet Another Slice of Fear". All received 5 Start reviews from Readers Favorite.

As Quality Leader and System Architect, Andrew's work gave him credit for a series of instructional manuals for site relationship management systems, various quality documents, and development lifecycles. In Andrew's spare time, he has a passion for many hobbies and his family, which he considers paramount. For more information about Andrew, please visit **andrewallensmith.com**.

Other titles available by Andrew Allen Smith:

The Masterson Files

    Vengeful Son
    Sinful Father
    Deadly Daughter
    Fateful Friend
    Silent Sister
    Curious Cousin
    Vengeance Incorporated **(2025)**

The Eternal Forever

    Adam
    Morgan (2025)

Slices of Fear

    A Slice of Fear
    Another Slice of Fear
    Yet Another Slice of Fear
    A Bigger Slice of Fear **(2025)**

Non-Fiction

    What NOT to say to People Who are Grieving
    How NOT to Grieve **(2026)**
    14 Stairs **(2025)**

Other Books

    A Slice of Passion
    Another Slice of Passion
    The Theft and Other Short Stories

Books containing the Work of Andrew Smith

    Simple Things
    A Portrait of Herbert Losch
    Monster Hunter Intern
    The Gift
    Pages Promotions: Chaos
    Pages Promotions: Madness

For more info or updated books lists visit:

andrewallensmith.com

www.ingramcontent.com/pod-product-compliance
Lightning Source LLC
LaVergne TN
LVHW051602080426
835510LV00020B/3092